DARTMOOR

First published in Great Britain in 1999 by
Colin Baxter Photography Ltd
Grantown-on-Spey
Moray PH26 3NA

A CIP catalogue record for this book is available from the British Library

ISBN 1-84107-039-4

Printed in Hong Kong

Front Cover Photograph: *Combestone Tor*
Back Cover Photograph: *Near Bowerman's Nose at dusk*
Page One Photograph: *Prehistoric stone row at sunset, Merrivale, near Princetown*
Page Three Photograph: *Vixen Tor, near Merrivale*

DARTMOOR

Photographs by LEE FROST

Introduction by IAN ROBINSON

Colin Baxter Photography, Grantown-on-Spey, Scotland

DARTMOOR
Ian Robinson

I was born in Devon at about the same time that the National Parks and Access to the Countryside Act was passed in 1949. A more significant event for me that year was my father abandoning me and vanishing for the next 40 years. My mother and her mother raised me, growing up beside the Exe, a powerful river that rises on Devon's other moor. In those televisionless days, Dartmoor and Exmoor were uncharted territory to a family without a car, imagined, rather than seen, through the exploits of Sherlock Holmes.

A treat in the spring of '56 was a charabanc outing from our seaside home to the wild heart of the county, a real expedition though, in truth, just a few miles beyond Exeter. It was my first encounter with the dark moor, creating the same indelible impressions that affect most newcomers. William Crossing, Dartmoor's famous writer, made mention of it as early as 1901. 'He [the newcomer] will realise that he has entered into a land different in every respect from that he has left behind'.

At Steps Bridge I well remember greaseproofed sandwiches among trillions of wild daffodils, while my shoes and socks dried after a dunking in the Teign. Then it was on to big, grey Hay Tor, and a long climb to lion-shaped rocks before a double ice cream cornet in the car park. The steep descent to Widecombe brought cream splits in the tea rooms, before my gastronomic tour of the moor was finally curtailed at Princetown. A cheeky pony stole my crisps through the doorway of the Railway Inn, in the days before cattlegrids stopped ponies invading the village (and kicking over the dustbins). As we boarded the homeward chara', I smiled for mum's Box Brownie to immortalize the day in front of the notorious prison, probably Dartmoor's best-known landmark. I don't remember if we stopped for fish and chips at Moretonhampstead, but nobody forgets the cold, gaunt gaol, least of all the inmates.

Originally built for French captives of the Napoleonic Wars in 1806, incarceration on the desolate moor was tough, so tough that a group of prisoners once seized the horse from a visiting refuse cart, hacked it to pieces and devoured it... raw! The prison was known as 'Halfway to Hell' in Victorian times. Today it might be England's Alcatraz with its daunting barrier of mists and mires that have foiled many an escape, some fatally. A Princetown friend said her father would bring the axes in from the shed when there was a breakout; others were known to put out a loaf and a pint of milk to deter a possible intruder.

At Grammar School, English lessons couldn't come quickly enough on Sherlock Holmes days. The pages of *The Hound of the Baskervilles* would suck us in like the lethal blanket bog that was the fictitious Great Grimpen Mire. Conan Doyle was actually inspired by Foxtor Mires that fringe the old Whiteworks mine south of Princetown. Finishing a recent walk in the pink dusk, I stopped gathering mushrooms to watch a wave of mist roll theatrically off Mount Misery. It swept into Sunshine Valley before levelling and lingering above the much documented mantrap that some call Dartmoor Stables, such is the mire's toll of ponies. Thickening with the fading light, the wispy fog clung and hovered around the spiky cottongrass, as if the bog were

Rippon Tor (opposite).

boiling. On the ridge it blurred the sharp edges of Fox Tor and obliterated the cross on the tomb of Childe, the unfortunate hunter who froze to death in a snowstorm. Folklore has it that he unwisely slew his horse, climbing inside its disembowelled carcase to keep warm.

Bounded by the A30 in the north and the A38 skirting the south, Dartmoor is the 368-square-mile granite dome in-between, 'like some fantastic landscape in a dream' according to Conan Doyle. It took 280 million years to evolve from molten magma to what guide books call 'the last great southern wilderness' that now attracts 10 million every year. Over the centuries, Nature's forces chiselled the sedimentary rocks to sculpt over 200 igneous outcrops, the tors that are Dartmoor's birthmarks. Like anything not flat on the planet, they have become magnets to man — the Celts called them *twrs*, or towers; the more accessible ones like Hound Tor, with its medieval settlements, have acquired 'honey-pot' status, while droves of pilgrims to Hay Tor are making it another Ayers Rock. Inevitably too, the tors have become the breeding ground of legends, on which Dartmoor thrives.

Massive Vixen Tor looms above the peat with an unmistakable outline resembling an Egyptian Sphinx. From a cave, the evil witch, Vixana, spun ensnaring mists to feed her black bog with the bones of unwary travellers. In the pastoral east, where the Webburn and the Bovey flow, witches were also responsible for the fate of poor Bowerman, a hunter who disturbed one of their ceremonies whilst chasing hares. They turned him into the pillar of granite that stands on Hayne Down and his hounds into the dog-shaped rocks at Hound Tor. The pixies, too, had a mischievous streak. To become disorientated and lose one's way on the moor equates to being 'pixie-led', from which the only escape was to quickly turn one's coat inside out! And there was

always the Devil to contend with. In 1638 lightning sent the tower on Widecombe's church crashing into the congregation, killing four; the Devil was blamed, allegedly for punishing card players in church. The cards are still to be seen in the shape of stone enclosures near Birch Tor, where the Devil threw them. Maybe too, his are the legendary 'Hairy Hands' said to grip steering wheels and send vehicles into the ditch on the road near Postbridge. A cleave nearby hides magical Wistman's Wood, a primeval forest of stunted oaks rising from a lichen-covered boulderfield, defying reason as to how they survive. Fragile veils of Spanish moss, as it's known in Louisiana, drape themselves from the bony-fingered branches, enhancing the mystique; shy adders bask there and some would have it that the Devil's hounds lurk around the gnarled trunks, eager for a kill.

Motoring across the moor in a downpour on a moonless night evokes eerie responses in the imaginative mind. Fog and clouds of rain engulf the car in an effort to suffocate it before the warm lights of the Two Bridges Hotel glow through rivulets on the windscreen. A saturated fox bravely evaded my wheels, dashing past headlights to the kitchen dustbins as I sought the sanctuary of a blazing log fire among the antiques. Easy to see why the place was so popular with Vivien Leigh, star of *Gone with the Wind*, and also with Edward and Mrs Simpson (who had connecting rooms). After a brief respite, the road beckons again; stay too long and they offer you a four-poster bed.

Winds bend the trees at Oakery bridge as deserted Princetown spreads below flashing lights on North Hessary Tor's giant TV mast; a yellow glow drenches the prison walls enclosing another sleeping world, before night closes in again at Devil's Bridge. New speed limits have recently civilised the moor, lending a fighting chance to huddled sheep, stubborn ponies and the tar-black Galloway cattle that materialise out of nowhere.

Descending Peak Hill, distant Plymouth glistens like an amber necklace. Old Brock the badger, just stepping out for the night, disappears clumsily into the tall hedgerow as lights go out in Walkhampton. One more village and I'm home, too.

As a young teenager I had my first walking experience of the moor joining a six-boy team on one of the first Ten Tors Expeditions, a 50-mile blood, sweat and cheers epic started by the Junior Leaders Regiment in 1960. Every spring, 2000 youngsters survive 36 character-building hours navigating between granite outposts in an endurance event of pride and pain comparable to the London Marathon. But in contrast to packed city streets, the little squads look vulnerable from afar in the sea of heather, criss-crossing the open moor on their separate quests. As I recall, it was more rain than shine, tough going for the untrained legs of a kid in his heavy, hob-nailed boots. Pumping an awkward Primus behind a granite windbreak brought little solace to the weeping blisters that precipitated my withdrawal after 35 tortuous miles. I was sad that I didn't get my medal; neither did Bobby Evans, who'd ballasted his rucksack with enough tins to feed a Scout troop! Modern rations are freeze dried, but Dartmoor's Atlantic storms don't alter; in 1996 a May blizzard forced the helicopter evacuation of large numbers, part of a massive recovery operation after the event was terminated early. 'In spate, five-foot streams become 15-foot brown torrents at 60 miles per hour that have to be ferried,' said a member of Dartmoor Rescue Group when everyone was safely accounted for. In the nineteenth century, the existence of this well-organised group of 200 volunteers might have prevented the tragedy documented on a Princetown gravestone. 'Three Valiant Soldiers of the 7th Royal Fusiliers lost in a snowdrift 12.2.1853'. In 1891, another blizzard buried the Yelverton to Princetown train for 36 hours, fortunately without loss of life.

To the walker, it becomes obvious that Dartmoor possesses a vast heritage of prehistoric remains; stone rows, circles, burial chambers and ancient settlements abound, going back to the Bronze Age. An axe head from the period was recently found on a public footpath near Postbridge. As durable as Time itself, granite monuments have withstood the elements; indeed, some are there because of them. A number of ancient ways are marked by standing stones or crosses – between Ashburton and Tavistock some are engraved A or T. Others are less well defined, like the Abbots Way that guided monks in all weathers past dangerous bogs between the abbeys at Buckfast and Buckland, or the Mariners Way, a well-trodden, 80-mile coast-to-coast path used by sailors 200 years ago to rejoin ships at Bideford or Dartmouth.

The early users of the plentiful granite knew it as moorstone. The Britons built hill-forts, then the Anglo Saxons left their mark with the first Dartmoor longhouses, sheltering livestock and owners under the same roof. It was a design that was to prove popular until the seventeenth century, and still survives around the moor. As demand increased for stone of specific dimensions, quarrying became necessary on a grander scale. With Scotland's granite the nearest equal to Dartmoor's quality, Devon became the obvious source for London's landmarks. The British Museum, Nelson's Column, many of the Thames bridges and New Scotland Yard all used the distinctive rock, much being conveyed from Haytor quarries behind 18 horses along flanged granite rails still in existence. Merrivale, Dartmoor's last granite quarry, supplied the Falklands memorial in Port Stanley. Now mothballed, the quarry's final order consisted of stone for office buildings at the Houses of Parliament.

My great-grandfather was a Cornish stonemason who helped cut the granite for Burrator dam, an impressive wall of dovetailed blocks that took five years to build and was intended to last as long as the hills. In those days, 'feathers' and 'tares' would have been his tools, ingenious devices used to split the rock with a hammerblow, leaving the distinctive indentations still visible on Dartmoor gateposts. Diamond-tipped saws and computerised thermal lances now do the job, slicing the granite like cheese. Burrator reservoir is a serene mile-and-a-half stretch of water that supplies 10 million gallons a day to Plymouth. On the wall of the dam is a commemorative tablet to Tavistock-born Sir Francis Drake; previously the city relied for three centuries on Drake's Leat, a water duct acclaimed as one of the sixteenth century's finest examples of engineering skill.

Not unlike a Scottish lochside, conifers as tall as rockets line the reservoir perimeter road, a Mecca for joggers and cyclists; discreet woodland trails sneak along the empty shoreline, passing the shell of an old manor that ivy has repossessed. Itinerant sheep scramble over moss-encrusted stone walls that have been there forever. The hopeful angler in waders and the buzzard wheeling over Down Tor are almost fixtures too, trying their luck at their respective predatory skills. Recent proposals to revamp and commercialise the location were dropped following vehement protestations by locals anxious to preserve its pristine charm.

The Great Western Railway once ran from Princetown, transporting quarried granite past the reservoir to Plymouth Sound and on to London via cargo schooners. My father spent some of his teenage years in a signalman's cottage there, watching locomotives and wandering beside the big lake. Now, track and trains have long been replaced by hikers on a panoramic walkway through some of the national park's best landscape. Rusting fenceposts made from Brunel's original railway lines are still visible beside obsolete bridges, but the whistle of the tank engine has given way to the songs of pipits and skylarks. By the old siding into Swell Tor quarry a dozen nine-foot corbels lie abandoned like beached whales, supports cut as spares for London Bridge in 1903, now doubly redundant since the bridge was moved to Arizona in 1970. Today, the buildings and equipment are no more; only telltale drill marks scar the sheer grey cliffs blasted by quarrymen. Ponies gambol recklessly across grassy tops, manes blowing in a wind that scours the ragged spoil tips, rubble fingers pointing forever at Walkhampton in the valley. When the mist is down you still think you hear the laden mineral train taking the curve from the sister quarry at Foggintor; strangely, the illusion persists as you scramble into the old workings, summoned by voices and the ghostly ring of steel on stone. There, across the flooded quarry, your senses are exonerated at the sight of climbing instructors encouraging belayed youngsters up the vertical granite for their Prince's Trust proficiencies.

In 1989 I returned from living in Alaska, America's 'Last Frontier', with the intention of finding my father, who I knew to be somewhere on the moor. Alaskans are not unlike Dartmoor folk, choosing where they live for the natural challenges and magic of a wild place. It was a momentous afternoon when I discovered him living fairly reclusively on an old mine, in a house that had seen far better days as a mine captain's prestigious residence in the nineteenth century.

West Wheal Robert, as the workings were known, produced almost 150 tons of copper in its best year, 1856, grossing over £13,000, easily enough to justify a big house. But mining was not for the faint-hearted; toiling long hours deep underground, be it for Yukon gold or Dartmoor tin, miners' perils were legion. Lit only by flickering candles stuck to their hats with clay, one

Combestone Tor (opposite).

man would rotate a hand bit whilst two others struck it with heavy hammers, making holes for the explosives. Blasting was done late, allowing the dust to settle before the morning shift began sorting. In 1886 disaster struck during fresh tunnelling in search of tin; a deluge of water burst through from older workings sending miners fleeing for their lives. Tragically, the mine captain and the carpenter didn't escape. In those hard times, if an accident didn't get you, then pneumonia frequently did.

Old mines still exist, though all are dangerous and usually sealed to public access. A geologist friend once took me below ground to an unlit world of bats and dripping passages. Stooping low and scrambling across boulderslides in the chilly darkness, we ventured cautiously along a disused tunnel, splashing through a muddy streambed where trucks once trundled. At one point he restrained me on the edge of a vertical shaft, an enormous hole through floor and roof that was used to take out the ore. (Momentarily, I remembered another guide's concern for my welfare when a large motionless snake appeared in the gloom of a Borneo cave!) Creeping gingerly around the precipice, we penetrated another 200 yards to an abandoned gallery; the beam from my caplight probed its inky blackness, highlighting pick marks where miners would have followed the lode bearing valuable cassiterite until it petered out, or they reached the surface. Exercising caution, we retraced our steps when rotting timbers holding back piles of waste rock inhibited further progress.

Hardly an acre of moor escaped the tinners over the last 800 years. Before the eighteenth-century miners, Elizabethans scarred the landscape with their gullies and tunnels. Sir Walter Raleigh, a Lord Warden of the Stannaries, called them 'the roughest and most mutinous men in England'. A law unto themselves, 96 representatives regularly convened the Stannary Parliament on top of Crockern Tor, overlooking busy medieval pack routes. It was chosen for its equidistance from the stannary towns, Tavistock, Chagford, Plympton and Ashburton, where the ore was taken to be assayed. Today, the Great Court of the Dartmoor Tinners is just a tranquil spot from which to gaze satisfyingly at hills beyond hills beyond hills; the trading routes have become the main roads that dissect the moor, bringing the local bus from Moretonhampstead, or horseboxes, European caravanners and inmates bound for Princetown. To the east, distinctive Bellever Tor now has a girth of mature conifers where you see deer at dusk; northwards, there's a red flag over Beardown Tor: the army is at play.

Neither plantations nor platoons are favoured by the conservationists though, arguably, the army's 150-year training tenancy on a third of the moor has managed to keep it open and available to recreationists. Now, sheep double for miners on Crockern's breezy summit as one tries to imagine the lawmakers' arguments that must have flown between its weathered slabs. The Stannary Court sat at Lydford, very infrequently. Transgressors unfortunate enough to alienate the tinners faced a wet cell in the castle and a rope's end next day, summarily seen off by notorious 'Lydford Law' – 'hang 'em in the morning, try 'em in the afternoon'.

Lydford's main attraction is its spectacular gorge; a rocky trail threads a deep wooded ravine where fiddleback ferns cling to impossible ledges above the fast moving River Lyd. Peat-brown water boils and batters itself through smooth rock bowls to end it all in a suicidal leap of virginal flume, the White Lady waterfall. Surefootedness is one's only caution now, unlike the days when the cave-dwelling Gubbins gang robbed, rustled and murdered in the locality. Gibbet Hill is a reminder of those lawless days, beside the Lydford road to Tavistock; the gallows may be gone but a historical monument close by is the restored Wheal Betsy engine house, where lead, silver and zinc were extracted.

A few winters ago *Trail* magazine asked me to walk the Two Moors Way, an odyssey of 102 miles across both Dartmoor and Exmoor. At short notice I did it in foggy February, when ponies that should be rocks confuse compass bearings and the heavy ploughed clay of mid Devon hampers your stride when the days are already short. Out of the country for five years, roaming the big spaces of North America, Dartmoor to a prodigal Devonian, was like discovering treasure in one's own back yard. The Two Moors Way gives a behind-the-hedges taste of Devon, a timeless cross-section of Dartmoor life, bracketed between Bronze Age settlements and quaint twentieth-century villages.

My favourite stretch crosses the black peat of wild Hameldown with its lonely barrows that only a compass can find on misty days. On others, when there's enough blue in the sky to clothe a navy, binoculars are mandatory for panoramas that defy infinity in every direction. Beyond the chequered fields of the Vale of Widecombe rise the familiar twin bosses of Haytor with the granite tramway following the contour, and the battlements of Hound Tor overshadowing distinctive Bowerman's Nose. Obvious Easdon Tor makes it easy to pick out Whooping Rock, where an infant could be cured of the cough by passing it through a granite hole. Untidily scattered are miniature sheep and cows, toy tractors and tiny tourbuses on ribbon roads that tie the whole scene together. The bright day highlights the gleaming white tower of Haldon Belvedere above Exeter; 20 miles beyond stand the pale cliffs of Branscombe and the Dorset coast. The thatched world of postcard Lustleigh hides in its sheltered cleave, except on May Day when the Queen is crowned with flowers on the granite throne in Town Orchard. My father spent his childhood there in the '20s – picnics at Becky Falls, roast chestnuts on the kitchen range, extra school milk allowance for his nosebleeds, apple picking, mum's whortleberry pies and sneaking rough cider from the barrel in the barn at Pullabrook Farm where they had a cider press. One could lose a whole afternoon up on Hameldown, hypnotised by the view from a heathered vantage point on a warm day; it takes a cloud blocking the sun to spur one back to the trail.

Fields of Devon red earth above Torbay's coastline fall away behind as you tread a wide, timeworn swathe through the heather towards Hameldown Beacon. Once on top, at 1697 feet, a very solid drystone wall pulls the eye right back down the next valley to Cator's patchwork oasis of pasture among the bleak moorland. Man has enjoyed these views for centuries; in 1872 Dartmoor's most significant archaeological find came off this ridge, an amber dagger pommel, inlaid with gold pins; sadly it was destroyed during the Plymouth blitz. The weathered wooden posts that seem to grow all across the high ground were a wartime deterrent against invading German gliders. Here too stands the RAF stone, a granite monolith bearing the squadron number and initials of four British airmen who crashed in 1941, returning from a mission over France. It seems curiously appropriate that modern airforce jets should skim over that same hilltop on daily training exercises to prevent another war like theirs.

We drop from Hameldown as we run the risk of inebriation with yet more majestic landscapes. Ahead lies Grimspound, a fairly large prehistoric settlement that was Conan Doyle's inspiration to bivouac Holmes in the remnants of a hut. It takes but a little imagination to add the poles and branches to the well-defined granite boundaries and you're looking at a Bronze Age community; my mind drifts to the ancient dwellings of the Anasazi Indians in Colorado as I climb, awed by Grimspound's spell, into the buffeting wind that haunts Hookney and Birch Tors, granite neighbours.

A fine monkey-puzzle tree betrays Headland Warren Farm;

where there was industry there was rabbit farming and the pillow mounds for breeding are as clear as the gullies belonging to Vitifer and Golden Dagger mines where toiling tinners would have excavated for the elusive lode. History seems to be everywhere on this hill. The dying sun highlights prehistoric reave lines, early field boundaries, and casts long shadows from stone row soldiers marching through the golden bracken. On the road, Bennet's Cross, a bent and weathered old man of granite, has been pointing the way to Chagford since the thirteenth century. For almost as long, wayfarers have sought hospitality at the nearby Warren House Inn, third highest pub in England, where they claim the fire's never gone out since 1845. When the building was resited, the embers were carried across the road on a shovel!

We pass within picnic distance of Fernworthy Reservoir's idyllic shores, then skirt Chagford to follow the banks of the dancing Teign through the grounds of Castle Drogo, England's last castle. Its mock medieval façade dominates a valley where deer roam unharrassed, whilst inside the granite parapets, a time warp of Edwardian splendour shows Edwin Lutyens at his best, the architect responsible for the Whitehall Cenotaph and for remodelling Lindisfarne Castle. Now cared for by the National Trust, Castle Drogo reflects the social standing of many that would flock to fashionable Chagford as a gateway to the moor, seeking respite from the smog-filled towns of the Industrial Revolution. Today the village's charm is preserved with its centre being a designated conservation area.

Thus dawned Dartmoor's tourism industry; James Perrott, a Chagford man, would guide Victorian clients across the exposed high moor where frequent driving rain and a bullying wind collaborate to soak the peat and scrub the granite. Army bunkers today prompt newsreel visions from the 1980s of 'yomping' Marines across identical Falklands terrain.

At Cranmere Pool, a particularly lonely spot, Perrott secreted a jar inside a cairn where his clients could leave cards, to be posted on by later visitors as proof that they had made the expedition to the remote heart of the north moor. Unwittingly, he conceived the pursuit of 'letterboxing', a passion akin to trainspotting that is unique to Dartmoor. A lot of walkers, armed with compass and cluebook, comb the national park seeking, not Munros, but containers that others have cunningly concealed behind marsh tussocks or among loose rocks that the locals call clitter. Inside is a visitors' book and a rubber stamp from which to swell one's personal collection. There are, apparently, thousands of boxes around the landscape, with stamps depicting all manner of Dartmoor facets, the industry, the wildlife, the people, the tors, the legends, even the prison. Twice a year, at the changing of the clocks, they have a big, slightly eccentric convention at Princetown to collect proficiency badges, promote charity walks and swap stamps and bog banter.

Whilst walking the Two Moors Way I encountered an old man ferreting patiently to and fro among the heather in the very loneliest of spots. He confessed to having had the letterboxing addiction for the past 30 years, with over 11,000 stamps in his book, and still searching! Parks policy is seemingly supportive or, at least, tolerant of this curious pursuit of gaining healthy exercise whilst discovering and appreciating Dartmoor. However, they do point out the need to be respectful of such things as ancient sites, private land and sensitive wildlife areas, and to observe all the rules of safety when venturing into the backcountry.

Widecombe-in-the-Moor (opposite).

Recently I was asked to compile a family bike ride for a guide book, incorporating the Plym Valley Cycle Way, Plymouth's avenue to the moor. The old railway viaducts provide splendid lookouts before riders are plunged into 80 yards of tunnel blackness, emerging to climb past sleepy Meavy with its ford and ancient oak on the green. The road follows the edge of Ringmoor Down where sons and dads fly kites way above chocolate-box Sheepstor village and the blue waters of Burrator. Living nearby, I pass the churchyard frequently. Suddenly, I'm looking at Kuching's blood-red sky staining the waters of the slow-moving Sarawak river, where sampan silhouettes are crossing to a dove-white palace, floodlit and gleaming in the balmy sunset. This splendid residence was built for a rajah, an English adventurer who became so involved with the affairs of a strife-torn Far Eastern country that he was asked to stay and rule in 1841. Sir James Brooke later retired to Sheepstor; his house bears a plaque and he is buried in the churchyard alongside his descendants, the 2nd and 3rd White Rajahs of Sarawak. The weathered granite church with its four crocketted pinnacles is pure Dartmoor; within, signatures in the visitors' book, a stained-glass window and bust of the much respected Rajah attest to strong links with Borneo, a country I know well. Sheeps Tor itself rises above, enhancing the timeless serenity; visible from Plymouth, $10^{1}/_{2}$ miles distant, it was used by men-of-war moored in the Sound in the nineteenth century, as a fixed point for compass correcting.

Walking the Two Moors Way in September would set one right for Widecombe Fair, one of England's best, and entrenched as deeply into Dartmoor life as tin mining ever was. A friend would walk there across Hameldown, dropping towards the tall church spires of the so-called 'Cathedral of the Moor' as fairground music rises through the purple and gold of the heather and gorse. Across the valley, a long snake of traffic is being swallowed by the village as it creeps down the vertical hill. Everyone is intent on having a good day out in the sunshine.

On the manicured village green a tattooed man collects fares for the big merry-go-round, surrounded by all manner of stalls – darts, hoop-la, household junk, candy floss and carved badgers, ponies and pixies. At the crossroads, a young vendor is barely visible under her canopy of unruly balloons. The main street, the only street, is thronging; the inn and the gift shops are overflowing, the Scouts have a bric-a-brac stall, a man is selling *Devon Life* magazine and in the village hall the ladies of the W.I. can't supply their pasties quickly enough. Crowds file past the Devon Air Ambulance stall on their way to the Fair Field, a Dartmoor shop window presided over by Uncle Tom Cobley on his traditional grey mare. Serious white-coated judges are studying masticating sheep for strong legs and good coats, undistracted by the clatter of highly polished vintage pumping engines. In the show ring, little girls of the Pony Club, watched by supportive mothers, are displaying Thelwell mares with fat bellies that almost touch the grass. Back at the horseboxes, older sisters are grooming Arabs for the showjumping in the afternoon; big brother is off admiring tractors with father... or in the beer tent. Everywhere you look, it's ribbons and rosettes, Land Rovers and Labradors, wellies, wax jackets, craftsmen and country folk. An old man in a shepherd's smock is thatching a hayrick, a shearer is deftly on his third sheep, while a stonemason demonstrates granite slicing with feather and tares – the attentive audience claps as the two slabs fall apart.

In the crowd, Germans and Americans can be heard as the Indian summer melts the leaden sky. The TV weatherman is downing a pint and watching the hounds from the local hunt grow bored, waiting for two massive Shire horses to leave the ring

— we're told they were ploughing by moonlight yesterday on a north Devon farm. Then, mid afternoon heralds the hilarious terrier racing, a berserk scramble in all directions as 20 out-of-control dogs of all shapes and hues pursue a dead rabbit, winched ballistically across the field on a rope. The terriers are a tough act to follow, but now it's the turn of the athletes who have meanwhile bussed to the top of the valley and are starting their hell-for-leather flying descent through fields, bogs, bracken and streams, back down to the main field. From the distant ridge, those paternal tors watch the mud- and blood-spattered finishers struggling home, looking down almost condescendingly as if to say, they've seen it all before.

Three weeks after the fair, Dartmoor life rolls on with the pony drifts, a sombre sight to behold.

The October sun is high in the sky, burning the haze from around Vixen Tor; there's nothing to indicate that this isn't just another tranquil moorland day. On Longash Common, a chaffinch is splashing in a stream, unperturbed by drinking sheep. As morning matures, cattle graze on but the ponies seem more active than usual, agitated. Beyond the stone rows a small group breaks into a canter down a slope towards the inn at Merrivale. Before long, more groups are moving across the open heath; something isn't quite right. It's as if a sixth sense is dictating their lemming-like direction, following the horse in front, but at the same time in flight, as if spooked by a moorland fire, but still no cause is evident to the observer. I move half a mile down the road to where I can see more coming off the ridgetop, herds now, streaming around the big grey tors and out on to the highway, pursued by a billowing dustcloud. Within a very short time the numbers build up until a whole flood of ponies is fast-trotting down the road, stopping traffic, gazes fixed, and silent, except for their clop-clop-clopping hooves on the spongeless tarmac. Among them a few innocent sheep have no option but to go with the flow, skipping to keep up. It's an arresting sight as they're driven, like refugees, *en masse*, to their unknown future; bays, greys, chestnuts, skewbalds, piebalds, duns, colts, fillies, mares, stallions, some proud, some scared, some lost, some confused, some no bigger than a large dog, all heading for the Dartmoor Inn in the coombe. A few let out a protesting whinny as they're herded into a stone-walled enclosure where they stand, tails flicking flies, awaiting the next move. The last stragglers come down the road looking almost apologetic for their lateness, followed by a dozen riders on healthy bloodstock. But for the little squad of noisy quad bikes bringing up the rear, this last roundup might have had a timeless air about it.

After the riders have had their beer and pasties the ponies are separated by brands as farmers claim their own; essentially, they're a cash crop allowed to roam all year until this day of reckoning. Now, they'll be sorted, with mares and fillies returning to the moor, but the future for most of the colts and stallions is less promising. They were once bred as pit ponies but the need isn't there any more. Auctions follow with a few going to private ownership, though, for most, it's a less dignified end as horsemeat or pet food. I watch in the afternoon glow as farmhands drive a herd home across the open moor, vanishing over the saddle between Ross Tor and Great Staple Tor in what, for many, will be their last gallop.

Within the week they're reluctantly spilling from cattle trucks to be herded into pens with an auctioneer's label glued to their rumps. The audience is mixed. The protection societies are looking for a rescue, farmers looking for a profit, meat men looking for a bargain, TV looking for an angle and jodhpurred youngsters looking for a pet. The system is not without its critics, though they say the trauma is considerably less than it used to be. '60 yer ago, a zucker would fetch five bob!' said an old farmer, pointing to a suckling foal. Each animal still has its moment of bewilderment in the sale ring before being dispatched to its fate for little more than a handful of guineas. 'What do they expect from us when they only fetch a few quid?' said another farmer.

And now, with a new century on the horizon, it's refreshing to see Dartmoor National Park's proposals, along with English Nature, for restoring and improving the fabric of the moor. Merrivale has just been designated the 4000th SSSI, due to its revealing landscape features from an era when reindeer and woolly mammoth roamed Dartmoor. Still talking pachyderms, the park has established an exchange link with a Nepalese national park that has an elephant breeding centre as well as a lot of similarities in terms of conservation and management. One might argue that this still doesn't extend far enough in comparison, say, with the USA, where the parks are little short of hallowed ground, but it's essentially one very significant step.

My father died in mid 1990; and so it was that I came to inherit a Listed dwelling in the national park, where buddles, launders and mineshafts are still to be found, relics of another era. His last letter to me described a severe January storm, illustrating the ferocity of Dartmoor's weather. 'The winds were recorded at 130mph… tearing huge holes in the roof… the ridge tiles came crashing down and straight through the bathroom… I was up in the loft at the time… I thought the whole roof was gone, it was deafening. Ivy and I were both very scared… My whole aim was to blank off the gaping holes to prevent the roof from lifting completely… that night I didn't see my bed until 3.30am.'

The ruthless temperament of Dartmoor is no secret, and particularly to farmers who will quote the local adage that is the moor's challenge: 'You scratch my back and I'll bleed you dry.' Echoing this, I remember the words of a man rearing beef and sheep on the unforgiving high moor. 'Granite soils are thirsty soils; 100 inches of rain washes all the value out of the ground and continually punishes the livestock. Dartmoor is like an inland island, a very hard place that makes farmers independent and self-reliant. You can't fight it, you roll with it like the sea; most learn the hard way.'

And yet, the continually changing weather is also Dartmoor's attraction. Its many moods, which isolate it from the rest of Glorious Devon, can swing from balmy to brutal in a very short time. Then, just as suddenly, the rain clouds lift and we're relieved to discover the sentinel tors still at their posts, guarding the heathery slopes and ferny hollows.

My father was off the moor for about 30 years, but it coaxed him back for his last 20. The elemental lifestyle becomes addictive to an outdoorsman. 'You get hooked on the wildness and the challenge,' confirms my farming friend, words I've heard so often in frontier Alaska.

William Crossing (1847-1928) probably best describes Dartmoor's inimitable spell:

'Those who have once set foot upon Dartmoor, who have climbed its giant tors, have listened to the plaintive music of its streams or have passed into its solitary places, where the cry of the curlew alone is heard, will, if they be true lovers of Nature, ever feel a longing to revisit it.'

Gems in a Granite Setting (1905)

Road to Postbridge at dusk (opposite).

Hound Tor (opposite).

Haytor Quarries (above).

Sharp Tor from Mel Tor (above).

Fingle Bridge and River Teign, near Drewsteignton (opposite).

Near Fernworthy Reservoir.

Prehistoric stone rows, Merrivale.

River Webburn in Great Lot Wood, near Buckland-in-the-Moor (above).
Ten Commandment Stones, near Buckland-in-the-Moor (opposite).

Looking towards Ponsworthy
from Bell Tor Corner (left).

Old door, Buckland-in-the-Moor (right).

Belstone Cleave,
Belstone, near Okehampton (left).

Bowerman's Nose,
an unmistakable landmark,
Hayne Down, near Manaton (right).

Stunted oaks, Wistman's Wood, near Two Bridges (opposite).

Combestone Tor (above).

Looking towards Walkhampton, near Yelverton at dusk (above).
Church of St Michael of the Rock, Brentor (opposite).

Bronze Age hut circle, Grimspound, near Manaton (opposite).
Drystone wall detail (above).

Poundsgate.

Pastoral Whitchurch Common, near Tavistock.

South of Okehampton Camp, near Okehampton (above).
Haytor Quarries (opposite).

Sunrise from summit of Brentor, near Tavistock (opposite).
Wild ponies at dusk (above).

Near Widecombe-in-the-Moor (above).
South of Okehampton Camp, near Okehampton (opposite).

Restored engine house, Wheal Betsy silver-lead mine on Black Down (opposite).

Saddle Tor (above).

Stormy autumnal scene near Haytor (above).

Dart Valley from Mel Tor (opposite).

Bell Tor (opposite).

White Lady Waterfall, Lydford Gorge (above).

Bennet's Cross on the Moretonhampstead to Postbridge road.

Near Widecombe.

Looking over to Hay Tor from Hound Tor (opposite).

Hound Tor at sunset (above).

Walkhampton Common (above).
Near Bowerman's Nose at twilight (opposite).

Looking across Cripdon Down at dusk (opposite).
Buckland-in-the-Moor (above).

Near Widecombe (above).
Granite detail, Hound Tor (opposite).

Queen's Silver Jubilee Memorial Stone, near Leusdon.

Looking across Yartor Down, near Dartmeet.

Burrator Reservoir from Sheepstor (above).
Bronze Age hut circle, Merrivale, near Princetown (opposite).

Hound Tor (opposite).

River Webburn and Buckland Bridge, near Buckland-in-the-Moor (above).

Haytor Quarries (above).
Merrivale at dusk (opposite).

Widecombe-in-the-Moor (opposite).

Stormy autumnal scene, Combestone Tor (above).

Sunset from Sharpitor, near Yelverton (above)
Near Postbridge at dusk (opposite).

Looking towards Sheepstor.

INDEX OF PLACES

LEE FROST was born in Barnsley, South Yorkshire, but spent the latter part of his teens living on the South Devon coast – which is how he came to discover Dartmoor. After spells as editor of *Photo Answers* magazine and assistant editor of *Practical Photography*, he was tempted by the freelance life and now divides his time between writing books on photography and contributing to one of Britain's leading picture libraries. His landscape and travel photographs have been published worldwide.

IAN ROBINSON is a freelance travel writer. He was born in Devon and lives on Dartmoor, but his work has taken him all over the world, to places as far apart as Mongolia and Borneo. His writing has been published in numerous outdoor magazines and in the national press.